The Satanic Praxis
Living the Narratives

Damien Ba'al

Published by Skeptic

an imprint of HLA Publishing LLC

Copyright © 2018 by Damien Ba'al

All rights reserved. Published in Hell by HLA Publishing LLC

hlapublishing.com

ISBN: 978-0-9986198-2-8

To everyone living the Narratives and putting together a culture of their own. This is for you.

Acknowledgements

Very special thanks to Wendy Ba'al for her love and support.

Thanks to Wendy Ba'al, Iris Shaw, and Riel Shower for help with the editing and revision process.

Thanks to Iris Shaw for the cover art.

Thanks to Tracey Pryor for the sigil of Baphomet.

Thanks to Khandnalie Barnes for all other sigils and symbols.

Thanks to Stephanie Cantrell for the alternate UAoS logo.

Contents

Prologue

I have discovered that people find a lot of meaning and fulfillment in ritual. I have also noticed that what already exists is not quite to my satisfaction. I would like to tighten the mythological symbolism, remove any woo, and increase the therapeutic effects.

For example, LaVey's main idea seemed to be releasing one's emotions, which is a valid psychological concept. I did not necessarily like everything though. I will be doing something fairly different here, but I will draw on a lot of the same concepts from psychology.

Meditation is another psychologically beneficial activity that is very ritualistic. There will be plenty of that here as well.

Much of this will be for the individual; things to be done alone. This is to be expected as Satanism and the Left-Hand Path are about individualism and the self. There will also be rituals to do with others, as well as some that are more ceremonial.

As usual, I will never say there is a "one true Satanism", or that things cannot be customized, or that this is the only way. I have a lot of ideas, but I do not presume to know everything. This is something that goes well with The Satanic Narratives, and I feel that it can be beneficial, fun, and add to our Satanic culture. Read on and try it out. See if this works for you as well.

Ave Satanas!

Commence the Praxis

Introduction

This is where one begins. I will go into detail about how these things are done, and start with some preliminary items. These are good starting points.

Everything in this book is meant to help people, and never to harm them. Do these things in moderation, keeping your health in mind. Never force anyone to do these things, as consent is always vitally important. Do not instruct your children to do these things. That is an abuse of parental power, particularly inappropriate with younger children who have not yet developed their reasoning ability. Furthermore, some items in here are not for children anyway.

If a child sees you doing some of the activities in here, and wants to join in, as children frequently do, treat it like you would cooking. You let the kids put an ingredient in a measuring cup, but not handle sharp knives or pull hot pans from the oven. You can let them sit with you without indoctrinating them with any ideas.

The main idea is never to do any harm. Do not force ideas on anyone; do not tell anyone what to think. Everyone needs to make an informed choice on their own and their wellbeing is important. Religious practices and psychological techniques have an abuse potential. I am strongly opposed to such abuse and harm. This should only ever be used to help, and enrich one's life experience.

When you go about following this guide, you may notice that there are times when you must refer to information in a different part of the book. You may also notice places where information repeats. This becomes most apparent in the praxis section that is divided by archetype.

Sometimes the information might be nearly identical other than one small piece. In that case, I refer you to an earlier section or two. Other times, the information may be partially the same, but have parts with significant differences. That is when some information will repeat in matching sections of the different aspects.

I try to strike a balance between repetition and having to skip around to different areas. I also want to make it as easy to pick an item and do it for each aspect in turn, as it is to focus on a single archetype, by doing everything for that particular aspect.

Meditation and Mindfulness

We will begin with meditation, which some may be unfamiliar with. It is not just for Buddhists, and there definitely will not be anything particularly Buddhist about it. Mindfulness meditation does not involve anything but clearing your mind and breathing. It is ideologically neutral.

Start by getting comfortable, and wearing soft, loose clothing, or even no clothing at all. Make sure you are in a quiet place free from distractions. You can skip this if you need to clear your mind for a few minutes while out, or at work, for example. However, when doing it for full effect in the home, comfort and environment are important.

Get in a comfortable seated position. You should be able to relax and let your muscles drain of tension and your body go mostly limp. Do not worry about any strict posture guidelines that you may have learned along with this. That is not important for what we are doing here.

When you are seated, close your eyes and breathe deep. Inhale deeply through the nose counting slowly to four, and then exhale through the mouth counting slowly to four again. Let all tension drain from your body as you do this.

After a minute or two, just breathe normally, in and out through the nose, count one and two going in, three and four going out. This should be slow and even. Concentrate only on the numbers and your breath.

After a couple minutes, you can stop counting. Just breathe in and out. Feel the air go in and out, from the movement in your chest to the air passing over your nostrils. Keep doing that for as long as needed. You may start with a few minutes, and later you might go longer. An hour is probably too much though.

While focusing on your breathing, keep your mind clear. When a stray thought wanders in, do not fight it, just go back to a clear mind. Treat the stray thought like a playful kitten. If the kitten jumps up where it should not be, you gently pick it, and place it back on the floor. Gently return your mind back to breathing in the same way.

When you are done, slowly open your eyes, let your mind do as it will, and orient yourself to your surroundings. Get up only when you are ready.

Throughout the day, you can do this while walking around. You can focus on your steps, and let your mind be empty. It can be like a reboot for the brain, leaving you refreshed when you engage your thoughts again.

You can also use this to help you fall asleep. Relaxation and clearing your mind can counter a number of obstacles that may prevent sleep.

Focus Meditations

The focus meditation is about getting in touch with your thoughts and feelings about a particular archetype. You focus on what the attributes of the archetype mean to you, how they affect your life, and how you might use them to your benefit. It can be about goal setting and self-improvement, or it can be about mental health. It is a focus on how you embody a set of archetypal attributes, and what those attributes do for you.

Each of the eight archetypes will have a focus meditation. The goal will be the cultivation and embodiment of the given attributes. It can also involve personal associations you have with a given archetype, which may be useful for you. Your individual praxis should be about you, and your wellbeing. It should be tailored to your particular needs.

There will be a praxis chapter for each archetype. In it, you will find the focus meditation. Each one will explain how it is done, and what the standard attributes are. Some attributes may be more relevant to you than others, and you may also have personal associations. This makes all eight of them very customizable.

Mantra Meditations

Each archetype will have a mantra meditation. It is very much in the spirit of the Vedic and Buddhist traditions. A mantra is a set of words or a phrase chanted aloud or in one's mind. It was frequently used by Buddhists to cultivate the qualities of different Buddhist figures. This was done through repetition of the mantra.

It is also used as a focal point to keep the mind occupied and focused during meditation. In mindfulness you want to see how the mind wanders and then go back to your breathing, but in mantra, you use the mantra to keep the mind focused.

In Satanism, it is much the same. We have archetypes, and can use a mantra to cultivate the attributes of a given archetype, in addition to keeping focus. To this end, I created a mantra for each. Each praxis will have a section with the mantra and pronunciation guide.

What follows are the instructions on how to perform a mantra. When you have selected a mantra and read the pronunciation guide, you may proceed. First, go to the next section, which is called "Ritual and Meditation Template".

Follow it through to step nine and then come back to these instructions. On step nine, go back to the mindfulness meditation section. Do the first part of that to begin. Keep going until you get to the part where the counting is done, and you are just following your breath. That is when you start with the mantra.

A mantra can be done aloud or internally. In addition to this context, you can recite a mantra internally during times of pain or anxiety to keep your mind off of it. Perhaps you are fearful of flying or needles. You can recite a mantra when taking off or getting blood drawn. Maybe you are experiencing something painful. Internally reciting a mantra can keep you from focusing on the pain, reducing how intensely you experience it.

In this context, when you reach the point of following your breath in meditation, begin reciting the mantra. If reciting aloud, begin with a breath and let it resonate deep in your chest. Let each time begin and end with each breath if at all possible. Ideally, you take a deep breath and then say it as you slowly exhale. Finish the mantra as you finish exhaling, but always let the mantra follow your breathing. Let the last sound of the mantra ring out and fade before beginning again.

Whether you do it aloud or internally, the mantra should fall in line with the rhythm of your breathing. Never change your breathing to fit the mantra. Keep that going the whole time you are doing it.

When you are finished, slowly let the mantra fade. This is more apparent when done aloud as the mantra fades in volume until you are silent and just back to breathing.

When you are done, slowly open your eyes, let your mind do as it will, and orient yourself to your surroundings. Continue with the remaining steps of the ritual and meditation template only when you are ready.

Ritual and Meditation Template

Other than the mindfulness meditation, I went over, and later meditations and rituals where I direct otherwise, everything will follow this general format. You will notice that the meditations presented, become incorporated in ritual this way, rather than being standard meditations. They are also, of course, Satanic in nature .

1) Dress, undress, or otherwise prepare yourself.

2) Prepare the location and bring any needed items.

3) Make sure it is quiet and that you will not be disturbed. Remove any distractions, if possible.

4) You can use candles, incense, or other items as desired. This can include an altar if you have one and any personal items you like to keep on the altar.

5) Get into a comfortable position, which may vary by ritual and preference.

6) Begin by ringing a bell. You can substitute a glass and silverware if needed. An electronic tone is also acceptable.

7) You will begin by saying something, like "hail Satan", "ave Satanas", or other words. Other aspects may be invoked, or an invocation may even be recited. This can depend on the specific ritual, or even personal preference.

8) Drink from a chalice/goblet/glass, whatever liquid you would like.

9) Do the specific ritual or meditation.

10) You may optionally drink again, if desired.

11) Ring the bell, or other object used at the beginning.

12) When the sound fades, say, "so it is done."

Progressibe Relaxation Ritual

This is not necessarily a ritual in and of itself, although it can be. This can be used in many different ways. You can do this entirely by itself, or by itself as step nine of the ritual and meditation template in the previous section. In either of those choices, you can add a visualization exercise, or you can go into some other ritual or some form of meditation.

This is a very modular component. You can combine it with various other things, in countless different ways. The most typical thing to do with it is add a visualization exercise afterward. You can create your own, or use one that is provided later in this book.

There will be a visualization ritual for each of the eight aspects. As part of that, it will instruct you to use the technique in this section.

You will either want to memorize these instructions or record yourself reading them aloud. At some point, you may even find recordings online of these being read. It is based on standard psychology, so it can be found outside the Satanic context as well.

You can do this sitting or lying down. For some purposes sitting may work better. However, for the best relaxation results, it is best done while lying down. I would recommend being on your back if possible.

Start by taking a few slow, deep breaths. Breathe in and then slowly exhale. This should be similar to the beginning of the mindfulness meditation, in an earlier section. After a few deep breaths, just relax and breathe normally.

You want to tense up all the muscles in your body slowly, counting from one to five. Then hold it for a couple seconds, and relax counting back from five to one. When you are relaxed, wait a few seconds before doing it again. I have found that going through this three times seems to be sufficient.

After the last time counting back down to one, just rest for a few seconds before continuing. Then you want to think of all parts of your body in turn, consciously relax them, feel them get heavy and sink into the surface, on which you are lying.

Start with your feet and ankles. Let them completely relax, and feel all the tension release. Next, relax the calves and lower legs, feel them get heavy and sink into the bed. Now let the relaxation move up to your knees and thighs, feel the tension release. Your legs should be very relaxed now. Let them get heavy and sink into the bed.

Feel the relaxation move up to the hips and lower abdomen. Many people clench the buttocks. Be sure to let those muscle relax completely, draining all tension. The muscles surrounding the genital area are frequently clenched as well. Be sure they are all completely relaxed.

Moving up higher let your abdominal muscles relax, then the back and the chest. Your entire torso should be free of tension now. Let your shoulders relax. Let them get heavy and sink into the bed. Let the relaxation continue into your arms and hands. Let them get heavy and sink into the bed.

The neck is an area where many people carry a great deal of tension. Be sure to let it relax and let your head sink into a pillow. The jaw is another area that is frequently clenched. Let it be slack. Let all the tension release.

Now let the rest of your head relax. The eyes and facial muscle should be still and have no remaining tension. Just stay in this relaxed state for a minute. Feel how it is to be completely relaxed throughout your entire body.

This is the point where you can slowly open your eyes, and be done with your session, or move on to the next thing. Or, if you are trying to get some sleep, you may begin to fall asleep now. You can also continue on to a visualization exercise.

If you are going to do a visualization exercise, you should have it selected already. If this is your first time reading through, I will include a short example here. You will also find one in each of the praxis chapters.

Imagine yourself at a beach. See the soft white sand, with water further out. Feel the sand under your feet, it is warm and gives a little as you step in it. You feel the warmth of the sun and a slow, cool breeze. There are sounds of seagulls chirping, and soft waves coming in to shore. The water starts out a rather green shade of blue. Then it gets more and more blue the further you look. It is a dark blue all the way out on the horizon.

That short example should give you a good idea of what the visualization is. There are eight full length ones in the Praxis section; one for each aspect.

The Invocation

This is something that can be said in place of a prayer, or just to open a meeting, or other occasion. It is general purpose.

With all of us present, so begins the invocation. Let us be the adversary of injustice, to think and question, never to blindly obey. If that makes us the outcast, so be it. We shall spread the light of knowledge and wisdom, and accept that light from others. Let reason guide our conscience to give us compassion and empathy for our fellow humans, to appreciate the earth, our home, and all the life upon it. Let each of us be a vital part of our community, as it transcends the sum of its parts, in emergence. Yet care for the self, to cultivate the light within. This is your power, without which, nothing is possible. Let us never lose sight of the joys of life, the pleasure of the moment—may it linger and spread. We fear not the chaos of life, but flow with it, to turn it in our favor. May it bring us only laughter. We do this in the name of humanity, for there is no other. It is up to us. So it is done.

The Invocation II

This is much like the first, but we add a harder edge to it. Some situations require the first one, but sometimes you can go all out with this one. The first is the original, while this one has been embellished.

Hails to all, infernal greetings! Ave Satanas! So begins the invocation. Let us be the adversary of injustice, to think and question, never to blindly obey. If that makes us the outcast, so be it. We shall spread Lucifer's light of knowledge and wisdom, and accept that light from others. Let reason guide our conscience to give us compassion and empathy for our fellow humans, to appreciate the earth, our home, and all the life upon it, in the balance of Baphomet. Let each of us be a vital part of our community, as it transcends the sum of its parts, in emergence as Leviathan. Yet care for the self, to cultivate the burning light of Belial within. This is your power, without which, nothing is possible. By the horns of Pan, let us never lose sight of the joys of life, the pleasure of the moment—may it linger and spread. We fear not the chaos of life, but flow with it like Loki, to turn it in our favor. May it bring us only laughter. We do this in the name of humanity, for there is no other. It is up to us. So it is done. Hail Satan!

𝕳𝖆𝖎𝖑 𝖘𝖆𝖙𝖆𝖓

Hail Satan, symbolic light,

metaphor of humanity.

An adversary among sheep,

an outcast and individualist.

Balanced with compassion,

and sense of community.

Wit, humor, carnal indulgence,

now until death, hail Satan!

The Reclamation of Reason

This is to help free you from childhood indoctrination. There can be lasting effects from such abuse suffered over years in childhood. This can be empowering, allowing you to come to terms with that, and to declare your freedom from their mental shackles. Some people might do a sort of "unbaptism", but that excludes people indoctrinated in other ideologies, and also grants a power and legitimacy to theistic religion, which it should never be given.

I find it better to reject outright, unfounded assertions on the nature of reality, arbitrary moral values, and the equally arbitrary authority on which it is based, as well as the supernatural entities around which such nonsense is formed.

This also affirms one's rational view on reality, and grounds moral codes in the normative values reached through the application of reason to the feelings evolved through group survival dynamics.

In the context of Satanism, this is done through the symbolism and iconography of metaphorical constructs, based on the mythologies relevant to our modern concept of Satan, the adversarial, archetypal figure.

The given name of "The Reclamation of Reason" does exactly that. The eponymous ritual will do likewise. This ritual should of course be fit into the context of the standard ritual format given in the previous section.

This ritual can be done alone or in a group, and even lends itself well to public display. When doing it alone, the items used, such as candles, incense, altar, and so on, should be customized to what you have and what has meaning to you. Meaning and purpose do not exist outside one's own subjective experience, and can only be provided by oneself. Direction from within is also the essence of the Left-Hand Path. Only you can know which items you need.

When this ritual is done for someone else, that person should provide these answers for the practitioner. The practitioner can help with examples and parameters though.

In a group this should incorporate the people both individually, and as a group. One may be more important than the other, for example, a chapter of a Satanist organization VS a group of random strangers.

In a group, presentation may be important. It is best to customize it to the group. The wearing of ritual robes or other attire, the location, and gestures used or other theatrics. It is only important to the presentation. The presentation can in turn affect the psychological effects, but only to a relatively small extent.

If you do this alone, you will probably read along silently, but say it aloud if that helps. You may go through the narration word by word, especially if you are unfamiliar. You may be doing this multiple times though, if you feel repetition will be helpful. In that case, you may simply do the given item, and not need to read the narration again.

In a group, and especially when doing a presentation, you may even feel the need to add to the narration a little. Whatever improves your performance is fine.

Do the steps in the ritual and meditation template, and then proceed to the ritual below, when you reach the appropriate step.

- As indoctrination is individual, you must think about what you were indoctrinated with. For Americans, this is almost certainly going to be a form of Christianity. Take a few moments to recall this in general. Keep this in mind as you continue.

- Initiations of different sorts are used in different ideologies. Baptism is a common example. Former Catholics may have Confirmation in addition. Your rational mind knows it is just a human being, the same as yourself, who performed this. You know it has no power over you—no power at all. It is symbolic only, so symbolically shall it be undone. Let the words and actions used to bind you to dogmatic superstition be undone. By your rejection and renunciation, so you are free.

- Wrath, punishment and torment are usually threatened. For most, it will be in the form of Hell. Your rational mind knows that no such thing can exist. It can haunt you just the same. Such concepts are abuse, used to coerce your obedience.

   Picture it as a place or collection of things— whatever works for your situation. See it get smaller and smaller. Watch it fade as it shrinks. See it get fainter and fainter. Let it keep getting smaller and fainter, until it is gone, without a trace.

   When it is gone, let yourself feel its absence. See how it feels for that to be gone, for the burden to lift from you.

- Purpose and meaning tend to be dictated by a deity. Think of the purpose and meaning forced upon your life. Think of something to symbolize this.

   Visualize this symbol in your mind. See it get smaller and smaller. Watch it fade as it shrinks. See it get fainter and fainter. Let it keep getting smaller and fainter, until it is gone, without a trace.

When it is gone, let yourself feel its absence. See how it feels for that to be gone, for the burden to lift from you.

Now realize that purpose and meaning do not exist outside of a mind. You create your own purpose and meaning. Let that creation of yours give you the best life you can build from your circumstances. Live your meaning and purpose forevermore.

- Shame and guilt are tools used by an ideology to control you. That goes along with the arbitrary moral code handed down by some supposed divine being. You will find that code is not very moral and neither are the shame and guilt that go with it.

Picture them in written form, like scrolls, tablets, or other objects that make sense for you.

Visualize this symbol in your mind. See it get smaller and smaller. Watch it fade as it shrinks. See it get fainter and fainter. Let it keep getting smaller and fainter, until it is gone, without a trace.

When it is gone, let yourself feel its absence.

See how it feels for that to be gone, for the burden to lift from you.

The guilt, shame, and arbitrary morality of a superstitious past are gone. Your rational mind knows that the wellbeing of humanity is the true basis of our moral feelings. Morality does not exist outside of the normative values of each subjective human experience. Live life on your own terms and by your own values.

- Gods or deities are the central part of most religions. There may be situations where this does not apply though. These powerful beings are supposed to be the source of everything. Yet there is no reason to think they exist at all. Your rational mind knows deities are a philosophical proposition, which is nothing short of ridiculous. The ones that are not logically impossible are unfalsifiable, and have been presupposed, with no possible source of knowledge other than the human mind. To put it simply, they are fictional. Visualize this fictitious being or beings in your mind. See it get smaller and smaller. Watch it fade as it shrinks. See it get fainter and fainter.

Let it keep getting smaller and fainter, until it is gone, without a trace.

When it is gone, let yourself feel its absence. See how it feels for that to be gone, for the burden to lift from you.

We are all that exist. We are the final authority and arbiter.

- All that ultimately came of this is ignorance and fear. Ignorance you have already conquered with knowledge. That knowledge and understanding is what brought you to this point. Now only the raw fear remains. For some it can rule your life, haunting you wherever you go.

  Now you can see that the source of the fear is gone. It no longer has any substance. Picture something that will symbolize this fear. Visualize this symbol in your mind. See it get smaller and smaller. Watch it fade as it shrinks. See it get fainter and fainter. Let it keep getting smaller and fainter, until it is gone, without a trace.

  When it is gone, let yourself feel its absence. See how it feels for that to be gone, for the burden to lift from you.

The fear has disappeared with the things that caused it. It has no power over you anymore. You can be at peace now.

- Reason has now been reclaimed. You are free of superstition and dogma. Hail Satan!

This is when you go back to the ritual and meditation template to complete this ritual.

Notes:

Notes:

Notes:

Notes:

𝕹otes:

The Praxis of Satan

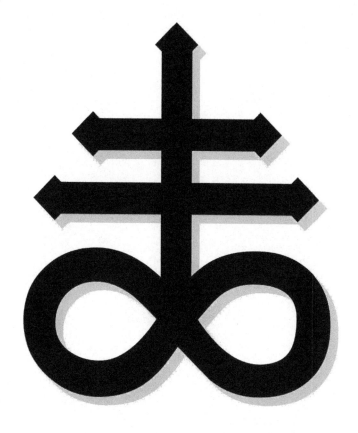

Invocation of Satan

Hail Satan! The adversary and accuser!
The eternal rebel, the everlasting question
Unswayed and Unyielding, to unjust authority,
To expectation and arbitrary social convention

The unbowed will, the strength within,
In forceful opposition to all oppression
Quislings quiver, and shills do shake,
When power crumbles, and tyrants fall

No dogma sacred, no tradition followed,
Through force of will, and action taken,
Let it be measured, and serve a purpose.
In the light of reason, Hail Satan!

Focus Meditation

The summary for the meaning of this archetype is: *Rebellion against arbitrary authority*

That is in the Purpose and Core Values statement, which is on the UAoS website and in United Aspects of Satan: The Black Book. You can get a better feel for it by reading The Invocation of Satan, earlier in this section. Even further information can be found in The Narrative of Satan, in The Satanic Narratives.

You might do this meditation just to cultivate these attributes in general, and possibly rotate through all the other archetypes as well. You might also do this for a more acute reason, like needing to be more assertive, or not allow an arbitrary social convention to hinder your happiness.

In this society, in which we live, there are these unspoken ways of doing things. You may know something is silly, and no one is standing over you enforcing it, but it was so drilled into you, that you cannot let it go. Indoctrination, whether religious or cultural, can be an unbreakable chain on your mind.

Break those chains. Break the ones binding your mind, and break the ones weighing it down with fear and guilt. Even when you are free to move, you may have quite a burden. Let that go by rejecting these arbitrary inhibitions that were dumped on you by caregivers.

That is a generalized example of one thing you might do. You can customize this to your particular needs. This is about you, your needs, and your life. However, even if you are not sure what you need, this can help.

By doing this with only the general attributes in mind, you become aware of your feelings in this regard, which will help you figure out what you need.

Start with the ritual and meditation template, going through to step nine. This meditation starts out like mindfulness.

Get in a comfortable seated position. You should be able to relax and let your muscles drain of tension and your body go mostly limp. Do not worry about any strict posture guidelines that you may have learned along with this. That is not important for what we are doing here.

When you are seated, close your eyes and breathe deep. Inhale deeply through the nose counting slowly to four, and then exhale through the mouth counting slowly to four again. Let all tension drain from your body as you do this.

After a minute or two, just breathe normally, in and out through the nose, count one and two going in, three and four going out. This should be slow and even. Concentrate only on the numbers and your breath.

After a couple minutes, you can stop counting. Just breathe in and out. Feel the air go in and out, from the movement in your chest to the air passing over your nostrils.

This is where you focus on your feelings, both in general, and how they relate to the archetype and its attributes. Keep doing that for as long as desired. You should start with only a few minutes and work your way up. It will not help to rush yourself.

When you are done, slowly open your eyes, let your mind do as it will, and orient yourself to your surroundings. Continue with the remaining steps of the ritual and meditation template only when you are ready.

Mantra of the Adversary

om hum satana ne

om=ohm

hum=hoong

hai=hi

i=ee

a=oh (cot) or uh (cut)

ne=nay

u=oo

satana=suhtohnuh

bakari=buhkohree

Invocation Ritual

For this ritual, you need an object like a stress ball, Chinese baoding balls, fidget spinner, or anything familiar to you. Some people might spin pens around, fold paper, bend paperclips, mindlessly doodle, anything like that is fine.

Start with the ritual and meditation template, going through to step nine. Start performing the standard action with your chosen object. Visualize an image of Satan. That is the primary archetype containing the others, much like you are contained by the space you occupy.

Focus on the space you occupy, and how its boundaries constantly change as you move. Feel that changing space as you perform the action. Now recite the Invocation of Satan, either internally or aloud. It is better if you have already recited the invocation on its own, so you are familiar with it. Let the rhythm of the words sync up with your movements.

When you finish the invocation (either the one time, or the number of times desired), let the last line fade, and then slowly stop the movements and visualizations. When you are done, continue with the remaining steps of the ritual and meditation template.

𝔙isualization 𝔕itual

Start with the ritual and meditation template. When you reach step nine, do the progressive relaxation ritual, and then proceed to the visualization ritual here.

Visualizations involve the imagination, but are usually about realistic situations—not always though. Many of them have the subject imagining themselves on a cloud that is rather bed-like. This will be much more fictional than usual.

Imagine that you find yourself light and slowly floating. An invisible bubble surrounds you. It is warm, protects you from the cold, radiation, and other dangers. The bubble has an endless supply of air. It moves by the power of your thoughts. You are floating up to edge of the atmosphere. You would begin to feel weightless, if you were not already weightless in your invisible, protective bubble.

You see the blackness of space, as you float out into the void. There is a satellite off in the distance, the international space station out beyond that. There are no sounds in space, so you hear only your own breath, going in, and then out, going in deeply, and then slowly back out again.

You feel only the sensation of your own body, and your breath going in and out. It is warm and relaxing as you float, safely in your invisible bubble. If you lit a candle or incense before your journey began, you will notice your experience is scented.

As you look back, you can begin to see more than just the earth. You are getting far enough away to see space appearing on the sides. You speed up greatly, but without any sensation. You are just traveling at speeds relative to the great distances between your destinations.

The moon is ahead of you, gray and pocked, like a giant battered boulder, hanging in space. You look back again to see the earth as a large blue and white orb. The planet that is your home is there, in its entirety, for you to see—getting smaller all the time.

You get a close view of the moon, to where it encompasses almost your entire field of vision. The rocky, uneven terrain is just coming into view. You linger a moment to take in the sight, then you are off in another direction.

The earth is now all you see, but it is small, like a large bluish marble. You glide through empty space in your bubble, by the power of thought. You see a reddish object come into view and get larger. It must be Mars. It is rather like the moon but with a brownish red tint to it. It is slightly less clear with its thin atmosphere. After moving in closer, and taking in the sight, you move off again—further out into space.

As you travel further and faster, you see the occasional rock off in the distance, in all different directions. The asteroids are all so very far away from each other, even here in this belt, that is packed in so relatively tight. Only the speed of your travels lets you see several of them.

Eventually you get a good look at Jupiter, a swirling ball of colors. It is like the colors of fall, with an ever-mixing palette of many different colors, going off at random, in all different directions. Faint flashes of light are just barely visible in the thick clouds.

You move on, ever further, out into space. You see the rings of Saturn coming into view. You pause and take in the colors, the glow and shimmer of the ice crystals. It all reflects the sunlight in so many beautiful ways. It is a mixed palette of summer and fall, the glimmering rings, with the swirling center.

The sun is small and faint, as you turn back toward home. It is like a soft nightlight out this far. Then by the power of thought, you are back to earth in a quick moment. You glide back into the atmosphere, your eyes close, your bubble disappears, and you feel yourself back where you were, before you went on your journey.

Slowly open your eyes and reorient yourself. When you are ready, continue through the remaining steps in the ritual and meditation template, in order to complete this ritual.

𝕹otes:

Notes:

Notes:

The Praxis of Ba'al

Invocation of Ba'al

Hail to the outcast! Ba'al the hated other,
The lone outsider, the one who perseveres
Eccentric in nature, unconventional in behavior
The one who is fallen, yet rises above all

When words are hollow, and deeds without reason
Validation becomes meaningless, approval is moot
Bask in the glow of their displeasure and scorn
Revive and recharge, renew and forever persevere

Free of it all, casting a shadow where you had been
The grass is greener, the air is sweeter and clear
Ba'al the hated other, the one who perseveres
Hail to the outcast! Hail Satan!

Focus Meditation

The summary for the meaning of this archetype is: *Perseverance in the face of opposition*

That is in the Purpose and Core Values statement, which is on the UAoS website and in United Aspects of Satan: The Black Book. You can get a better feel for it by reading The Invocation of Ba'al, earlier in this section. Even further information can be found in The Narrative of Ba'al, in The Satanic Narratives.

You might do this meditation just to cultivate these attributes in general, and possibly rotate through all the other

archetypes as well. You might also do this for a more acute reason, like other people picking on you or your friends, or perhaps you have a difficult obstacle to overcome.

There is that voice in the human mind that tells you that you cannot, that you must give up. We have tendency to feel as if we cannot do this or that. If that is borne out by evidence, you may want to listen, but usually it is the voice of fear and self-doubt. It may be the only thing holding you back.

Doubt is wonderful when it is rational, but sometimes it is not. Do not doubt anything out of hand, or in the face of evidence. Doubting your abilities before you try is failure by default. While you should not embark on a fool's errand, do not concede as failure that which is unknown and untested.

In empirical matters particularly, failure is the first step of knowledge. Do not be afraid to fail, and thereby learn how to succeed. Instead, persevere in the face of opposition. Either you succeed, or you gain valuable insight and information. Only giving in to irrational doubts leads to true failure.

That is a generalized example of one thing you might do. You can customize this to your particular needs. This is about you, your needs, and your life. However, even if you are not sure what you need, this can help.

By doing this with only the general attributes in mind, you become aware of your feelings in this regard, which will help you figure out what you need.

Start with the ritual and meditation template, going through to step nine. This meditation starts out like mindfulness.

Get in a comfortable seated position. You should be able to relax and let your muscles drain of tension and your body go mostly limp. Do not worry about any strict posture guidelines that you may have learned along with this. That is not important for what we are doing here.

When you are seated, close your eyes and breathe deep. Inhale deeply through the nose counting slowly to four, and then exhale through the mouth counting slowly to four again. Let all tension drain from your body as you do this.

After a minute or two, just breathe normally, in and out through the nose, count one and two going in, three and four going out. This should be slow and even. Concentrate only on the numbers and your breath.

After a couple minutes, you can stop counting. Just breathe in and out. Feel the air go in and out, from the movement in your chest to the air passing over your nostrils.

This is where you focus on your feelings, both in general, and how they relate to the archetype and its attributes. Keep doing that for as long as desired. You should start with only a few minutes and work your way up. It will not help to rush yourself.

When you are done, slowly open your eyes, let your mind do as it will, and orient yourself to your surroundings. Continue with the remaining steps of the ritual and meditation template only when you are ready.

𝕸antra of the 𝕺utcast

ah om ba'ala hum

om=ohm

hum=hoong

hai=hi

i=ee

a=oh (cot) or uh (cut)

ne=nay

u=oo

satana=suhtohnuh

bakari=buhkohree

𝕴𝖓𝖛𝖔𝖈𝖆𝖙𝖎𝖔𝖓 𝕽𝖎𝖙𝖚𝖆𝖑

For this ritual, you need an object like a stress ball, Chinese baoding balls, fidget spinner, or anything familiar to you. Some people might spin pens around, fold paper, bend paperclips, mindlessly doodle, anything like that is fine.

Start with the ritual and meditation template, going through to step nine. Start performing the standard action with your chosen object. Visualize an image of Ba'al. Ba'al came from an ancient sky god, and was the Lord of Flies.

Feel the air around you, and concentrate on the air going in and out of your lungs. You breathe in, and then out again. Now recite the Invocation of Ba'al, either internally or aloud. It is better if you have already recited the invocation on its own, so you are familiar with it. Let the rhythm of the words sync up with your movements.

When you finish the invocation (either the one time, or the number of times desired), let the last line fade, and then slowly stop the movements and visualizations. When you are done, continue with the remaining steps of the ritual and meditation template.

𝕭isualization 𝕽itual

Start with the ritual and meditation template. When you reach step nine, do the progressive relaxation ritual, and then proceed to the visualization ritual here.

Visualize yourself floating in the sky. You glide on a warm breeze over to a big, white cloud. The cloud looks very soft, and you sink into it a little, when you lie on it. It is like the softest bed you have ever felt. You are practically weightless. If you lit candles or incense, that scent swirls through the air around you.

You feel warm and comfortable, sinking into the fluffy cloud. All you hear is your breath going in and out, breathing in deeply, and slowly exhaling. You feel your breath going in and out, as you are partially enveloped by the soft, silky cloud.

The other clouds float by, at their own lazy pace, taking their time, wafting along on the gentle breeze. You feel comfortable and safe on your cloud. You are in solitude there, but quite content, and able to go back whenever you wish.

It is nice to have some time to yourself, escape the busied hurry of your day, and take a break from all the people. You have time to be you, to relax there on your soft cloud, and be alone with your thoughts—or even take a break from your thoughts too.

Just feel your breath go in and out, as you relax there on your cloud. Breathe in and then breathe out again. Keep focusing on that as you float on your cloud. Spend a few more minutes like this. If you record this, perhaps set a timer with it, or add something soothing to the recording for the desired period of time. You may also find this good for falling asleep.

Slowly open your eyes and reorient yourself. When you are ready, continue through the remaining steps in the ritual and meditation template, in order to complete this ritual.

Notes:

Notes:

𝔑otes:

The Praxis of Lucifer

The Praxis of Lucifer

Invocation of Lucifer

Hail Lucifer! Bringer of knowledge and wisdom!
The light bearer, skeptic and critical thinker,
The bright, shining light, illuminating all
Dispelling the darkness of ignorance and superstition

The mental spark, and focused reason
The thirst for knowledge, and how to know
Lies are revealed, and faith is destroyed
No gods survive, no magic remains

Skeptical inquiry, an understanding shared,
Reality laid bare, humanity on its own,
No idea beyond question, no authority absolute,
Hail Lucifer the light bearer! Hail Satan!

Focus Meditation

The summary for the meaning of this archetype is: *Scientific and philosophical skepticism*

That is in the Purpose and Core Values statement, which is on the UAoS website and in United Aspects of Satan: The Black Book. You can get a better feel for it by reading The Invocation of Lucifer, earlier in this section. Even further information can be found in The Narrative of Lucifer, in The Satanic Narratives.

You might do this meditation just to cultivate these attributes in general, and possibly rotate through all the other

archetypes as well. You might also do this for a more acute reason, like learning more about critical thinking, or dissecting an argument.

Obviously, study is by far the best way to achieve this, but this meditation may aid you in those goals. At the very least, it could open your mind and give you ideas.

That is a generalized example of one thing you might do. You can customize this to your particular needs. This is about you, your needs, and your life. However, even if you are not sure what you need, this can help.

By doing this with only the general attributes in mind, you become aware of your feelings in this regard, which will help you figure out what you need.

Start with the ritual and meditation template, going through to step nine. This meditation starts out like mindfulness.

Get in a comfortable seated position. You should be able to relax and let your muscles drain of tension and your body go mostly limp. Do not worry about any strict posture guidelines that you may have learned along with this. That is not important for what we are doing here.

When you are seated, close your eyes and breathe deep. Inhale deeply through the nose counting slowly to four, and then exhale through the mouth counting slowly to four again. Let all tension drain from your body as you do this.

After a minute or two, just breathe normally, in and out through the nose, count one and two going in, three and four going out. This should be slow and even. Concentrate only on the numbers and your breath.

After a couple minutes, you can stop counting. Just breathe in and out. Feel the air go in and out, from the movement in your chest to the air passing over your nostrils.

This is where you focus on your feelings, both in general, and how they relate to the archetype and its attributes. Keep doing that for as long as desired. You should start with only a few minutes and work your way up. It will not help to rush yourself.

When you are done, slowly open your eyes, let your mind do as it will, and orient yourself to your surroundings. Continue with the remaining steps of the ritual and meditation template only when you are ready.

Mantra of Wisdom

hum dige duta nu

om=ohm

hum=hoong

hai=hi

i=ee

a=oh (cot) or uh (cut)

ne=nay

u=oo

satana=suhtohnuh

bakari=buhkohree

Invocation Ritual

For this ritual, you need an object like a stress ball, Chinese baoding balls, fidget spinner, or anything familiar to you. Some people might spin pens around, fold paper, bend paperclips, mindlessly doodle, anything like that is fine.

Start with the ritual and meditation template, going through to step nine. Start performing the standard action with your chosen object. Visualize an image of Lucifer. Lucifer is the angel of light, the morning star.

Focus on your consciousness itself. Be aware of everything from your breath to your movements, almost perceiving your perception itself. Now recite the Invocation of Lucifer, either internally or aloud. It is better if you have already recited the invocation on its own, so you are familiar with it. Let the rhythm of the words sync up with your movements.

When you finish the invocation (either the one time, or the number of times desired), let the last line fade, and then slowly stop the movements and visualizations. When you are done, continue with the remaining steps of the ritual and meditation template.

Visualization Ritual

Start with the ritual and meditation template. When you reach step nine, do the progressive relaxation ritual, and then proceed to the visualization ritual here.

You are walking down a hallway toward a big set of wooden, double doors. It is a quiet hallway, mostly empty. The double doors at the end are still a ways off. You pass the occasional door off to one side or the other.

You feel your feet pressing against the floor with each step. You hear your footsteps and your breath. You breathe in and out as you stroll down the hall, getting nearer to the doors at the end.

When you reach the doors, you see they are decorative, polished, and rather antique looking. They feel heavy as you push them open. You walk through the doorway into a very large library. There are shelves of books everywhere, as far as the eye can see.

Once you have pushed the doors back to their closed position, you turn back to face the library. You are in a decorative entranceway with a shining marble floor. You walk onto the thin carpet of the library, looking around at all the different rows of shelves. You see the occasional person here and there, but there are very few people, and it is quite a large building.

You continue on past rows of shelves into a different wing of the library. It seems almost entirely empty and even quieter. You hear your soft footsteps, your breathing, quiet whispers and the occasional soft rustle of paper back behind you.

You reach rows of shelves and begin walking between two long rows of shelves. It must be half the length of a football field, with occasional spaces on either side. They are quite high too. You would have to stretch to reach the top shelf.

All the books around you are older and bound in leather. It all seems very clean—no dust anywhere. You continue walking until you can see where the shelves end. It looks like some sort of a study or sitting area. You continue walking along the shelves.

When you reach the end, you walk out from between the shelves and into small cozy little area. There are a couple desks and an oblong table with a few chairs. There are also leather armchairs with end tables and a coffee table. The lighting is soft and easy on the eyes. There are a couple of lamps in the area. There is a very large Persian rug going across the floor.

You walk past the decorative desks, and over to one of the big comfortable, oversized armchairs. You sit in it, and feel almost like a kid because of how big it is. It feels very soft as you sink into the cushion a little. It is relaxing sitting in the big suede leather chair.

It is peaceful and quiet as you sit there in the chair, looking out into the library. There are so many rows of shelves, and each row is quite long. You sit there for a while, enjoying the relaxing atmosphere of the library. Stay as long as you desire.

Slowly open your eyes and reorient yourself. When you are ready, continue through the remaining steps in the ritual and meditation template, in order to complete this ritual.

Notes:

Notes:

𝕹otes:

The Praxis
of Baphomet

Invocation of Baphomet

Hail Baphomet! Horned God, Goat of Mendes!
As above, so below, man and woman, dark and light
Self-motivation balanced with,
compassion and reason in all things

The nature of reality is shit happens
Adrift in a chaotic universe, without purpose
In this place of nihilism and chaos
The only meaning is that which we create

Breasts so soft, and a shaft of steel,
Hair, horns, and hooves, with flapping wings
Two finger up, two fingers down
As above, so below, Hail Baphomet! Hail Satan!

𝔉𝔬𝔠𝔲𝔰 𝔐𝔢𝔡𝔦𝔱𝔞𝔱𝔦𝔬𝔫

The summary for the meaning of this archetype is: *The use of logic, reason, and empirical evidence to shape our morality*

That is in the Purpose and Core Values statement, which is on the UAoS website and in United Aspects of Satan: The Black Book. You can get a better feel for it by reading The Invocation of Baphomet, earlier in this section. Even further information can be found in The Narrative of Baphomet, in The Satanic Narratives and United Aspects of Satan.

You might do this meditation just to cultivate these attributes in general, and possibly rotate through all the other archetypes as well. You might also do this for a more acute reason, like trying to work out an ethical decision.

Your feelings on the matter, which are the essence of conscience, can be better accessed in this way. These moral feelings work in conjunction with reason to make a decision.

That is a generalized example of one thing you might do. You can customize this to your particular needs. This is about you, your needs, and your life. However, even if you are not sure what you need, this can help.

By doing this with only the general attributes in mind, you become aware of your feelings in this regard, which will help you figure out what you need.

Start with the ritual and meditation template, going through to step nine. This meditation starts out like mindfulness.

Get in a comfortable seated position. You should be able to relax and let your muscles drain of tension and your body go mostly limp. Do not worry about any strict posture guidelines that you may have learned along with this. That is not important for what we are doing here.

When you are seated, close your eyes and breathe deep. Inhale deeply through the nose counting slowly to four, and then exhale through the mouth counting slowly to four again. Let all tension drain from your body as you do this.

After a minute or two, just breathe normally, in and out through the nose, count one and two going in, three and four going out. This should be slow and even. Concentrate only on the numbers and your breath.

After a couple minutes, you can stop counting. Just breathe in and out. Feel the air go in and out, from the movement in your chest to the air passing over your nostrils.

This is where you focus on your feelings, both in general, and how they relate to the archetype and its attributes. Keep doing that for as long as desired. You should start with only a few minutes and work your way up. It will not help to rush yourself.

When you are done, slowly open your eyes, let your mind do as it will, and orient yourself to your surroundings. Continue with the remaining steps of the ritual and meditation template only when you are ready.

Mantra of Balance

ah bakari sira hai

om=ohm

hum=hoong

hai=hi

i=ee

a=oh (cot) or uh (cut)

ne=nay

u=oo

satana=suhtohnuh

bakari=buhkohree

Invocation Ritual

For this ritual, you need an object like a stress ball, Chinese baoding balls, fidget spinner, or anything familiar to you. Some people might spin pens around, fold paper, bend paperclips, mindlessly doodle, anything like that is fine.

Start with the ritual and meditation template, going through to step nine. Start performing the standard action with your chosen object. Visualize an image of Baphomet. Baphomet stands for balance, of both opposites, and any set of components.

The universe around you is chaos, yet your consciousness, awareness, and intentionality, exist by bringing those different pieces of the chaos into balance. Feel that balance as you perform the movements, and feel how the movement itself is balanced. Now recite the Invocation of Baphomet, either internally or aloud. It is better if you have already recited the invocation on its own, so you are familiar with it. Let the rhythm of the words sync up with your movements.

When you finish the invocation (either the one time, or the number of times desired), let the last line fade, and then slowly stop the movements and visualizations. When you are done, continue with the remaining steps of the ritual and meditation template.

Visualization Ritual

Start with the ritual and meditation template. When you reach step nine, do the progressive relaxation ritual, and then proceed to the visualization ritual here.

You are on an alien world. It must be a large moon with an atmosphere. You feel much lighter, just a little more than half your usual weight. You are standing on something resembling short grass and clover, but it is an orange brown color, and covers the ground. It feels about room temperature and there is a light breeze at your back.

Everything has a reddish tinge, including the sky and the sparse clouds. It is dim like the soft lighting of a room made for relaxing. To the right there is a small, red sun. It appears to be half the size of the sun on earth. However, it must be a fraction of the size, but much closer. You can feel some warmth from the sunlight.

To your left, there is an enormous, multi-colored object taking up almost the entire sky in that direction. It appears to be a gas giant planet. It has swirling colors of fire and earth tones. The colors are a little dull and subdued, but the patterns are pleasing, like an abstract painting.

You walk forward, with a sun to your right and a planet to your left. Trees dot the landscape—or at least they look like trees. They look similar to palm trees in some ways, but they curve and bend a little more. There are some bushy orange and brown leaves at the top, but no branches.

The air smells like incense, or maybe some sort of candle. It is very quiet. You can hear your breathing a little, and your faint, soft footsteps. The leaves of the trees do not move much with the light breeze, so there is no rustling.

It is the most relaxing walk you can remember taking. Yet at the same time, the unusual scenery is exciting. Just breathe in deeply, and then slowly breathe out again. Then take a few minutes to just look around, see what is there. You might find something else that is interesting. Alternatively, you can just relax for a while, and enjoy the pleasant day. Take your time and enjoy before you leave.

Slowly open your eyes and reorient yourself. When you are ready, continue through the remaining steps in the ritual and meditation template, in order to complete this ritual.

Notes:

Notes:

Notes:

The Praxis
of Leviathan

Invocation of Leviathan

Hail to The Leviathan! The beast of the sea!
The water of life, the creative community
From communal emergence, and combined expertise
Powerful adversary, aggregate of our strength

Individual efforts, an emergent force
Molding reality, shaping our destiny
From out of the black flame they appear
Your brothers and sisters in rebellion

Down the individual, winding paths
There is a convergence, and the dragon arises
Into the water, the beast of the sea
Hail to The Leviathan! Hail Satan!

Focus Meditation

The summary for the meaning of this archetype is: *Community for the creative freedom and betterment of every person*

That is in the Purpose and Core Values statement, which is on the UAoS website and in United Aspects of Satan: The Black Book. You can get a better feel for it by reading The Invocation of Leviathan, earlier in this section. Even further information can be found in The Narrative of The Leviathan, in The Satanic Narratives.

You might do this meditation just to cultivate these attributes in general, and possibly rotate through all the other archetypes as well. Friendships and other relationships are all about feelings. Therefore, the possibilities are endless with this particular aspect.

You can customize this to your particular needs, and even if you are not sure what you need, this can help.

By doing this with only the general attributes in mind, you become aware of your feelings in this regard, which will help you figure out what you need.

Start with the ritual and meditation template, going through to step nine. This meditation starts out like mindfulness.

Get in a comfortable seated position. You should be able to relax and let your muscles drain of tension and your body go mostly limp. Do not worry about any strict posture guidelines that you may have learned along with this. That is not important for what we are doing here.

When you are seated, close your eyes and breathe deep. Inhale deeply through the nose counting slowly to four, and then exhale through the mouth counting slowly to four again. Let all tension drain from your body as you do this.

After a minute or two, just breathe normally, in and out through the nose, count one and two going in, three and four going out. This should be slow and even. Concentrate only on the numbers and your breath.

After a couple minutes, you can stop counting. Just breathe in and out. Feel the air go in and out, from the movement in your chest to the air passing over your nostrils.

This is where you focus on your feelings, both in general, and how they relate to the archetype and its attributes. Keep doing that for as long as desired. You should start with only a few minutes and work your way up. It will not help to rush yourself.

When you are done, slowly open your eyes, let your mind do as it will, and orient yourself to your surroundings. Continue with the remaining steps of the ritual and meditation template only when you are ready.

Mantra of Friendship

om sapa pani di

om=ohm

hum=hoong

hai=hi

i=ee

a=oh (cot) or uh (cut)

ne=nay

u=oo

satana=suhtohnuh

bakari=buhkohree

Invocation Ritual

For this ritual, you need an object like a stress ball, Chinese baoding balls, fidget spinner, or anything familiar to you. Some people might spin pens around, fold paper, bend paperclips, mindlessly doodle, anything like that is fine.

Start with the ritual and meditation template, going through to step nine. Start performing the standard action with your chosen object. Visualize an image of Leviathan. The Leviathan is the beast of the sea. It is the water of life.

Be aware of the water that makes up most of your body. Feel your heart beating as it circulates in your blood. Now recite the Invocation of Leviathan, either internally or aloud. It is better if you have already recited the invocation on its own, so you are familiar with it. Let the rhythm of the words sync up with your movements.

When you finish the invocation (either the one time, or the number of times desired), let the last line fade, and then slowly stop the movements and visualizations. When you are done, continue with the remaining steps of the ritual and meditation template.

𝔙isualization 𝔕itual

Start with the ritual and meditation template. When you reach step nine, do the progressive relaxation ritual, and then proceed to the visualization ritual here.

You are walking on a white, sandy beach. It is a warm day, with a cool breeze, and the sun is shining. You feel the sand under your feet, a little hot, but tolerable for walking. The waves are gently crashing into shore, and you hear seagulls overhead. The light smell of the sea reaches you, as you walk toward the water.

You see the water roll in, and then wash back out again. It seems to follow the pattern of your breathing, coming in and then going back out again. The water gets more and more blue, the further out to sea you look.

The sun feels warm on your skin, as you are cooled by the breeze coming in from the sea. You continue walking across the beach, heading out toward the shore. You have a raft tied up there. When you get near it, you untie the rope, and walk to the raft with it.

The raft has a sail and a paddle on it, but is otherwise just a flat raft, about fifteen feet across. It is moving out to sea a little, but you pull it back with the rope.

Your feet are now on wet sand. It is cool, and squishes under your toes. The water feels cool as well, as it washes over your feet, and then goes back out again. The raft is bobbing a little with the waves.

When you get close enough to the raft, you wait for the water to go out, and then you take a couple running steps, and then leap onto the raft. You pull the rope in and toss it off to the side. The raft starts to drift slowly out to sea, as you sit down.

Once you are a few meters out from the shore, the waves become a gentle up and down motion. Occasionally a little water reaches the surface of the raft, flows across, and drains back into the sea.

It is nothing but water in front of you, as far as you can see, all the way out to the horizon. It is just peaceful and relaxing. You gently bob up a little, and back down again. It matches the rhythm of your breath, breathing in, and then back out again.

You let the raft drift out until it reaches the deeper water, where it has the darker blue color. Then you open the sail, let it catch the breeze, and gently push you back toward the shore. It is not a very strong breeze, so the raft moves slowly, and gently bobs up and down in the mild waves.

Breathe in deeply and back out again, as you float back to shore. Relax and enjoy floating on the raft for a few more minutes.

Slowly open your eyes and reorient yourself. When you are ready, continue through the remaining steps in the ritual and meditation template, in order to complete this ritual.

Notes:

𝔑otes:

Notes:

The Praxis of Belial

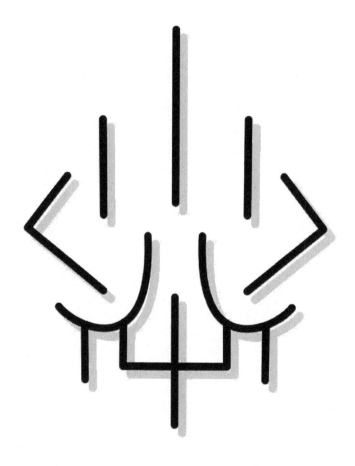

Invocation of Belial

Hail Belial! Hail to the individual, and thyself!
Anthropomorphic symbol of the Left-Hand Path
It is the self, an inner journey
To know one's mind, conscious and unconscious

Independent thought, leave the herd behind
Self-discovery, understanding, your inner calm
The black flame, lighting the dark path
always self-directed, and truly unique

Never conforming or contrarian, or externally directed
Never emulation of an in-group, playing to a stereotype
Internally motivated, manifestation of will
Hail Belial! Hail to thyself! Hail Satan!

Focus Meditation

The summary for the meaning of this archetype is: *Individualism and individual accomplishment*

That is in the Purpose and Core Values statement, which is on the UAoS website and in United Aspects of Satan: The Black Book. You can get a better feel for it by reading The Invocation of Belial, earlier in this section. Even further information can be found in The Narrative of Belial, in The Satanic Narratives.

You might do this meditation just to cultivate these attributes in general, and possibly rotate through all the other archetypes as well.

Meditation is very much about the self, which is the essence of this aspect and the Left-Hand Path. Any feelings that come up at all can be useful here. It is about cultivating a sort of love and respect for yourself, and the introspective part of the Left-Hand Path journey.

This is one of the best ways to explore the self, gain understanding, and find fulfillment. This allows you to connect with your feelings, which will help you figure out what you need.

Start with the ritual and meditation template, going through to step nine. This meditation starts out like mindfulness.

Get in a comfortable seated position. You should be able to relax and let your muscles drain of tension and your body go mostly limp. Do not worry about any strict posture guidelines that you may have learned along with this. That is not important for what we are doing here.

When you are seated, close your eyes and breathe deep. Inhale deeply through the nose counting slowly to four, and then exhale through the mouth counting slowly to four again. Let all tension drain from your body as you do this.

After a minute or two, just breathe normally, in and out through the nose, count one and two going in, three and four going out. This should be slow and even. Concentrate only on the numbers and your breath.

After a couple minutes, you can stop counting. Just breathe in and out. Feel the air go in and out, from the movement in your chest to the air passing over your nostrils.

This is where you focus on your feelings, both in general, and how they relate to the archetype and its attributes. Keep doing that for as long as desired. You should start with only a few minutes and work your way up. It will not help to rush yourself.

When you are done, slowly open your eyes, let your mind do as it will, and orient yourself to your surroundings. Continue with the remaining steps of the ritual and meditation template only when you are ready.

Mantra of Self

ah bali'ala hum

om=ohm

hum=hoong

hai=hi

i=ee

a=oh (cot) or uh (cut)

ne=nay

u=oo

satana=suhtohnuh

bakari=buhkohree

Invocation Ritual

For this ritual, you need an object like a stress ball, Chinese baoding balls, fidget spinner, or anything familiar to you. Some people might spin pens around, fold paper, bend paperclips, mindlessly doodle, anything like that is fine.

Start with the ritual and meditation template, going through to step nine. Start performing the standard action with your chosen object. Visualize an image of Belial. Belial is of the fire element, or energy.

Be aware of the energy of your body. The energy released from chemical reactions in your cells, as it changes to the heat of your body. It is also transferred, in kinetic form, to the object you are moving. Now recite the Invocation of Belial, either internally or aloud. It is better if you have already recited the invocation on its own, so you are familiar with it. Let the rhythm of the words sync up with your movements.

When you finish the invocation (either the one time, or the number of times desired), let the last line fade, and then slowly stop the movements and visualizations. When you are done, continue with the remaining steps of the ritual and meditation template.

𝔙𝔦𝔰𝔲𝔞𝔩𝔦𝔷𝔞𝔱𝔦𝔬𝔫 ℜ𝔦𝔱𝔲𝔞𝔩

Start with the ritual and meditation template. When you reach step nine, do the progressive relaxation ritual, and then proceed to the visualization ritual here.

You are in a clearing, right in front of a forest. You walk down the beginning of a path, leading in. You are on a dirt path, with trees on either side of you. The leaves are thick and green overhead, letting in only scattered dots of sunlight here and there.

There is an earthy smell, and the fragrance of plant life. Birds are chirping in the treetops above, and the occasional rustle from small animals, scurrying through the shade plants and fallen leaves. A long way down the path, a family of deer runs across, disappearing into the trees on the other side.

There are many different kinds of trees, both young and old. Some trees have vines, and some are even covered in moss. You feel at peace among the trees, walking down the path between them.

You hear the sound of running and trickling water. As you walk further along, you see a creek up ahead. It is a very small creek. It is only a couple feet wide, and a foot deep in the middle. There is a little mud on either side as well, so you start running, and then leap across the creek.

It was fun and exhilarating jumping across to the other side. You are breathing a little heavier, your heart beating faster now. You soon relax again, as you walk down the path.

The path winds around in one direction, and then back in the other. You eventually come to large partially hollow log off to the side. You walk over to it, and then sit down.

You sit on the log, just enjoying the peaceful and relaxing woods. You look around at all the different trees for a while. Then you are just still. In that moment, you are in the perfect place to be.

Breathe in deeply and then back out again. Enjoy the peaceful forest for a few more minutes or perhaps a little longer.

Slowly open your eyes and reorient yourself. When you are ready, continue through the remaining steps in the ritual and meditation template, in order to complete this ritual.

𝕹𝖔𝖙𝖊𝖘:

Notes:

𝕹otes:

The Praxis of Pan

Invocation of Pan

Hail to Pan! Hail to the pleasures of life!
The horned god, patron of the carnal world
Cloven hooves travel all the paths to joy
Making the most of one's only life

Whether sensual and sexual, visual or auditory
A gustatory delight, or cerebral ecstasy
Your unique subjective experience, one performance only
Maximizing the opportunity, with all you enjoy

Never wasting or depriving, abstaining or sacrificing
Never holding out for lies, or spiritual pipe dreams
embracing the here and now, celebration and indulgence
Hail to Pan, archetype of pleasure! Hail Satan!

Focus Meditation

The summary for the meaning of this archetype is: *Indulgence in the pleasures of life*

That is in the Purpose and Core Values statement, which is on the UAoS website and in United Aspects of Satan: The Black Book. You can get a better feel for it by reading The Invocation of Pan, earlier in this section. Even further information can be found in The Narrative of Pan, in The Satanic Narratives.

You might do this meditation just to cultivate these attributes in general, and possibly rotate through all the other

archetypes as well. You might also do this for a more acute reason, like feelings of guilt or shame surrounding the activities you enjoy.

Our cultures (both with and without religion) seem to indoctrinate us with ideas of pleasure and indulgence being wrong. It can be like this in any area, but it is the most pronounced in sexual matters.

Even after breaking free from harmful ideas, the effects may persist. When you feel guilt and shame needlessly, it can hinder what you do. Let these feelings surface and see if they can be dealt with. Try to build acceptance for who you are and what you enjoy.

That is a generalized example of one thing you might do. You can customize this to your particular needs. This is about you, your needs, and your life. However, even if you are not sure what you need, this can help.

By doing this with only the general attributes in mind, you become aware of your feelings in this regard, which will help you figure out what you need.

Start with the ritual and meditation template, going through to step nine. This meditation starts out like mindfulness.

Get in a comfortable seated position. You should be able to relax and let your muscles drain of tension and your body go mostly limp. Do not worry about any strict posture guidelines that you may have learned along with this. That is not important for what we are doing here.

When you are seated, close your eyes and breathe deep. Inhale deeply through the nose counting slowly to four, and then exhale through the mouth counting slowly to four again. Let all tension drain from your body as you do this.

After a minute or two, just breathe normally, in and out through the nose, count one and two going in, three and four going out. This should be slow and even. Concentrate only on the numbers and your breath.

After a couple minutes, you can stop counting. Just breathe in and out. Feel the air go in and out, from the movement in your chest to the air passing over your nostrils.

This is where you focus on your feelings, both in general, and how they relate to the archetype and its attributes. Keep doing that for as long as desired. You should start with only a few minutes and work your way up. It will not help to rush yourself.

When you are done, slowly open your eyes, let your mind do as it will, and orient yourself to your surroundings. Continue with the remaining steps of the ritual and meditation template only when you are ready.

Mantra of Pleasure

om khusi anada nu

om=ohm

hum=hoong

hai=hi

i=ee

a=oh (cot) or uh (cut)

ne=nay

u=oo

satana=suhtohnuh

bakari=buhkohree

Invocation Ritual

For this ritual, you need an object like a stress ball, Chinese baoding balls, fidget spinner, or anything familiar to you. Some people might spin pens around, fold paper, bend paperclips, mindlessly doodle, anything like that is fine.

Start with the ritual and meditation template, going through to step nine. Start performing the standard action with your chosen object. Visualize an image of Pan. Pan is carnal like the earth. It is like the physical matter of your body.

Focus on the physicality of yourself. You have size, weight, density. Be aware of your physical form as you continue performing the movements. Now recite the invocation of Pan, either internally or aloud. It is better if you have already recited the invocation on its own, so you are familiar with it. Let the rhythm of the words sync up with your movements.

When you finish the invocation (either the one time, or the number of times desired), let the last line fade, and then slowly stop the movements and visualizations. When you are done, continue with the remaining steps of the ritual and meditation template.

𝔙isualization 𝔚itual

Start with the ritual and meditation template. When you reach step nine, do the progressive relaxation ritual, and then proceed to the visualization ritual here.

You are in a meadow. The grass is a deep green, and the terrain is flat, with few trees. To your left is a hill leading up to a roadway, to the right and behind you is a large forest. Up ahead is a rocky area with hills leading to a small mountain you can see off in the distance.

The sun is on your back, just a couple hours before it sets. It is a pleasant temperature, and the winds are calm. It is very quiet, and the smell of fresh grass hangs in the air. All you can hear are some birds chirping in the nearby forest.

You are calm and relaxed as you breathe in and out. You breathe in deep and then slowly back out again. The meadow is peaceful, as you enjoy the fresh air and the singing of the birds. You keep walking through the meadow, soaking it all in.

After a few minutes, you reach a more rocky area. You can hear the faint sound of rushing water, and you see a cave ahead. The mouth of the cave is tall and wide. You continue walking toward it, as the sound of rushing water gets closer.

When you reach the cave, you can see clearly into it. The sun is getting lower in the sky and shining right into the cave. You can see occasional stalagmites and stalactites further back. You walk inside, and the air feels cooler as you go. It seems to slope downward as you go back—the ceiling more than the floor.

When you get a little further, you can see the water. It is flowing from the back of the cave coming in your direction, but is going down underneath you. There must be a stream that runs down from the mountain and under the meadow. The water is clear and sparkling, as it flows along its path.

You stand for a while listing to the rushing sound, watching the stream flow. It is cool and peaceful in the cave, with an earthy smell, and only the sound of water in your ears. You breathe in and then back out again, as you relax and enjoy.

Watch the stream for a few more minutes, taking in the calm. Then you can come back, when you are ready.

Slowly open your eyes and reorient yourself. When you are ready, continue through the remaining steps in the ritual and meditation template, in order to complete this ritual.

Notes:

𝔑otes:

𝕹otes:

The Praxis of Loki

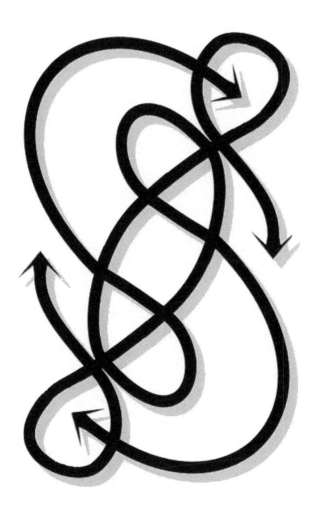

Invocation of Loki

Hail Loki! Hail to the archetype of cunning and humor!
The trickster and the joker, prankster and clown
Always underestimated, but several steps ahead
Rational genius cloaked in the madness of a fool

From tricks and traps to satire, farce, and lampoons
Misdirection and the unexpected, accompanied by laughter
Never on the straight path, always twisting and turning
Round and round, then back again, like a giant knot

Destruction of pomposity, not even leaving dignity
Serious goals, from silly pranks, chaos reigns
See fascists and theocrats hoist on their own petard
Hail Loki, archetype of cunning and humor! Hail Satan!

Focus Meditation

The summary for the meaning of this archetype is: *The application of humor, fun, wit, and cunning in our endeavors*

That is in the Purpose and Core Values statement, which is on the UAoS website and in United Aspects of Satan: The Black Book. You can get a better feel for it by reading The Invocation of Loki, earlier in this section. Even further information can be found in The Narrative of Loki, in The Satanic Narratives.

You might do this meditation just to cultivate these attributes in general, and possibly rotate through all the other

archetypes as well. That is what I would recommend with this particular aspect. The feelings you find when exploring this will be unpredictable, which is to be expected.

Start with the ritual and meditation template, going through to step nine. This meditation starts out like mindfulness.

Get in a comfortable seated position. You should be able to relax and let your muscles drain of tension and your body go mostly limp. Do not worry about any strict posture guidelines that you may have learned along with this. That is not important for what we are doing here.

When you are seated, close your eyes and breathe deep. Inhale deeply through the nose counting slowly to four, and then exhale through the mouth counting slowly to four again. Let all tension drain from your body as you do this.

After a minute or two, just breathe normally, in and out through the nose, count one and two going in, three and four going out. This should be slow and even. Concentrate only on the numbers and your breath.

After a couple minutes, you can stop counting. Just breathe in and out. Feel the air go in and out, from the movement in your chest to the air passing over your nostrils.

This is where you focus on your feelings, both in general, and how they relate to the archetype and its attributes. Keep doing that for as long as desired. You should start with only a few minutes and work your way up. It will not help to rush yourself.

When you are done, slowly open your eyes, let your mind do as it will, and orient yourself to your surroundings. Continue with the remaining steps of the ritual and meditation template only when you are ready.

Mantra of Chaos

ah om galata hum

om=ohm

hum=hoong

hai=hi

i=ee

a=oh (cot) or uh (cut)

ne=nay

u=oo

satana=suhtohnuh

bakari=buhkohree

Invocation Ritual

For this ritual, you need an object like a stress ball, Chinese baoding balls, fidget spinner, or anything familiar to you. Some people might spin pens around, fold paper, bend paperclips, mindlessly doodle, anything like that is fine.

Start with the ritual and meditation template, going through to step nine. Start performing the standard action with your chosen object. Visualize an image of Loki. Loki is the aspect of chaos, much like our chaotic universe.

Consider that only a mind with intentionality brings the kind of order we understand. Outside of that, there is only matter obeying physical laws. Everything is otherwise in chaos. Now recite the Invocation of Loki, either internally or aloud. It is better if you have already recited the invocation on its own, so you are familiar with it. Let the rhythm of the words sync up with your movements.

When you finish the invocation (either the one time, or the number of times desired), let the last line fade, and then slowly stop the movements and visualizations. When you are done, continue with the remaining steps of the ritual and meditation template.

𝔙isualization 𝔕itual

Start with the ritual and meditation template. When you reach step nine, do the progressive relaxation ritual, and then proceed to the visualization ritual here.

You are standing in front of a large mirror. It is not a normal mirror. The surface seems to ripple like water, but it does not appear to be a liquid. This is actually the mirror of chaos, which will take you to a random place, unless you picture somewhere you want to go.

You will stay where the mirror takes you, until you feel like it is time to return. Then you will be back in front of the mirror again.

Now you must make a choice. Either picture a place you want to go, or clear your mind completely. Get your mind into the desired state. When you are ready, step through the mirror.

You are now on the other side of the mirror. Where are you? Is it random, or did you choose this? Look around on all sides. What do you see around you? Are there any sounds to be heard? What are you hearing right now?

Are you inside or out? Is it warm or cool, and is there a breeze? Does the air smell of anything? How do you feel about being here? Do you know why you are here?

It could be that this is a place for you to relax. Or, maybe your mind is trying to tell you something. It could be different every time you do this. You are bound to get different results by choosing a place than by letting it be random.

It is possible that you tried for a random place and ended up nowhere. You might be in a world of nothingness. You may have to try again, or choose a place for now. The mirror relies on your state of mind to work.

Take a little time to figure out where you are and why, if you are not sure. That would be something good to explore. If you are somewhere nice, spend some time here. Just relax for a while and enjoy yourself.

When you feel like you are ready to go, you will find yourself in front of the mirror again. You can always try again right away if someone is there with you. Otherwise, open your eyes slowly, get reoriented, and set your recording to play again-unless of course, you memorized this. Continue until you are finished, and back in front of the mirror for the final time this session.

Slowly open your eyes and reorient yourself. When you are ready, continue through the remaining steps in the ritual and meditation template, in order to complete this ritual.

Notes:

Notes:

𝕹otes:

The United Aspects
of Satan

Meditation of the Eight Infernal Aspects

For this meditation, we derive an element from each aspect. Pan is very physical, so it is the earth element. It represents solid matter. Leviathan is obviously water. Ba'al is air as it was a sky god. Belial is associated with fire, so it is the element of fire or energy.

Lucifer the light bearer represents consciousness. Since Satan is both the adversary aspect and the summation of the aspects, it represents space. It is sort of a container for the aspects. So, it represents the space taken up by physical objects.

Baphomet is balance and order. It is your consciousness making sense of the world. It is your meaning and purpose. Loki is chaos. It is the way the universe seems from our perspective.

This meditation goes one by one through the elements represented by the aspects. One meditates on their place in the universe. For example, you start with Pan, the physical, earth element. You think about the physical matter of the universe, how some of it currently makes up your body, that it had been in a different form, and that it will be in yet another form in the future.

You go through this, as directed for all the elements. You can take as much or as little time as you want for each one. The first time through, you can just read along and think about it without actually doing the meditating. Then, when you remember how each part goes, you can do the meditation without needing to read along with it. Another option is two people guiding each other through it.

Start with the ritual and meditation template. When you reach step nine, do the mindfulness meditation as laid out in the first section. When you reach the main stage where you are focusing on your breath with a clear mind, do that for a couple minutes and then proceed to the meditation of the eight infernal aspects.

It begins with Pan, and the earth element. As you meditate, focus your mind on your physical being—the solidness of your body, skin, muscle, bones. It is all made of atoms that used to be parts of various other things. They have been recycled and reformed many times. Many of them were forged in the heart of massive stars, or during supernovae.

They will become other things again. Your skin cells flake off, muscle cells die and are replaced. Your bones are dissolved and rebuilt little by little over time. It is easy to consider your physical body as part of the universe.

Next is Leviathan, and the element of water. A large portion of your body is water. It makes up the blood that flows through you. It is involved in all the functions of your body. You constantly cycle fluid in and out of your body.

Fluid is mixed into most organic solids, and even in the air. It evaporates, condenses, and soaks into something else. The cycle never ends.

Ba'al represents the air element. You feel it circulating around you. You breathe it into your lungs and then back out again. It is with you briefly, and then gone again moments later.

It is almost incorporeal, yet stars begin as massive clouds of gas. They collapse under gravity until the atoms are fused together.

Belial is associated with fire or energy. You can feel the heat of your body. Consider the food you take in. It is turned into fuel in a chemical process. It is converted from a chemical energy into kinetic energy in your cells. It powers your body, allowing you to move.

Satan represents space. You are always taking up space. It is never the same space though. You are constantly moving. The earth is also rotating, and orbiting the sun.

Even the sun is moving, going around the galaxy, revolving around a large black hole in the center. You never take up a given space for more than an instant.

Lucifer is your consciousness. It is your thoughts and feelings. It is the thing that is most definitively you. Even your thoughts come and go though. As abstract and complex as it is, your consciousness is of the material universe. It is just the effect of your intricate networks of brain cells working together.

Your consciousness is you, yet it is of your brain, obeying the laws of physics. There is not a point where the material universe ends and your essence begins.

Your consciousness puts everything in balance, making order from a chaotic universe. Baphomet is balance, or more accurately order, in this context. This is the part of your mental processing that provides meaning and purpose to your life.

There is no meaning, purpose, or morality to the universe. Only your conscious mind can provide that. Your mind is of the universe, but it requires your thought processes to provide these things.

Putting the chaos of the universe into balance, results in the creation of your subjective experience. You can only understand reality through this subjective experience, and it is what lets you perceive meaning and purpose as something more significant than other thoughts.

Even this subjective experience, that perceives who you are, and the nature of objective reality, is just a part of consciousness. That in turn is produced by the physical brain, made of the same matter as everything else.

Loki is the chaos of the universe. From your perspective, it seems to be chaos. Your mind turns it into order. However, even the chaos of the universe only seems chaotic on our macro scale. At the particle level, it is merely obeying the laws of physics.

It is predictable in theory, but in practice, the prediction would equal the mass and energy of the universe. Therefore, it is ultimately determinate. Yet it appears to be indeterminate due to the physical limitations of such perception.

As you have meditated on each of these elements in turn, you can see how they are all definitively you, yet just pieces of the universe at the same time. It is all the same, all the material, carnal world. The difference is only the ability to think and perceive, and all that goes along with that.

Now clear your mind and just breathe for a minute or two. Relax, breathe in, and back out again. Pause here for as long as is needed. You may even need a little time for reflection.

When you are done, slowly open your eyes, let your mind do as it will, and orient yourself to your surroundings. Continue with the remaining steps of the ritual and meditation template only when you are ready.

Ritual Customization

Even with the more general form that the rituals take in this book, there is room for customization. Those tend to be for chronic ongoing situations, or generally to improve one's mental wellbeing. It is not so easy to deal with acute situations though.

If I make a ritual for getting over the end of a relationship, that is very specific. It is one of many forms of loss and grieving. Yet it is also including so many different possibilities. Every relationship is different. Each person tends to prefer dealing with it in a different way depending upon their personality. Therefore, even making one specific to relationships would require a great deal of customization, and still leave the need for many other rituals, just for loss and grieving alone.

Dealing with loss and grief is a category that encompasses many things. It is also only one of many such categories. The experience of life is far too complex to simplify with a book of some cookie-cutter remedies.

This is also in the context of Satanism. If it is anything, Satanism is a set of philosophies that prominently feature individualism. Thinking for yourself, and being able to customize tools is part of being a Satanist. Likewise, you expect and demand a philosophy that emphasizes self-direction, and provides easily customizable tools in anything that dares to be called Satanism.

This is a tool that can be customized to any situation in which one may end up. You can design whatever ritual you like, for a given situation.

Like almost everything in this book, this is done as the ninth step of the ritual and meditation template.

To create your ritual, start by writing down how you feel. Perhaps even do one of the meditation rituals to help you figure that out.

What are some items that provide symbolism to the situation and how you feel about them? Write down as many as you can.

What actions would you perform that relate to this? Would some actions be symbolic? Would some actions be repetitive and calming? Write these down.

What are some items you would need for the actions? Write down whatever comes to mind.

What are some words you want to say or think? Anything you want to visualize? Write these down as well.

Read over what you have written and give it some thought. After thinking about it, go through and delete anything that will not work, or set it aside for later use with something else. Mark some ideas as maybe. Add anything that comes to mind while doing this.

Go through it again and try to finalize the list. Know which items are needed for actions and which are more symbolic. Figure out the actions you want to perform, and in what order.

What about the words and visualizations? How do those fit in with the actions and items? Do you need to do some editing and rearranging?

Put it all together into a complete ritual where it is clear what you need, and lays out everything you will say and do. Read over it to make sure it is right, and then do some editing to come up with a finished customized ritual.

This is your personal step nine for the particular situation you are in right now. Go through all the steps of the ritual and meditation template with this as your ninth step.

You should feel empowered to create anything you need to help you get through whatever life throws at you. Each one you create will be easier than the last, complexity notwithstanding of course.

Notes:

𝕹otes:

Notes:

Ceremonies and Group Rituals

Introduction

The ceremonies can be used as they are or customized. They are written with the United Aspects of Satan in mind, but can be adapted for anything. They cover the typical milestones of life. These are the same ones mentioned in The Satanic Narratives.

The announcing is for expectant parents. It is short, so you are best to combine it with something else. The Welcoming is for anyone having a baby. It is along the same lines as Secular Humanist welcoming ceremonies.

The Transitioning could be considered the Satanic Bar/Bat Mitzvah, but not really. The differences greatly outnumber the similarities. It does happen at thirteen though. The Becoming is about reaching physical adulthood, becoming a full member of the United Aspects of Satan, and each day becoming a better person than the day before. It is done at eighteen. The Joining is for new members who want to have a ceremony.

The Wedding is pretty obvious. The Ending is like a funeral, but it focuses on celebrating and commemorating a life.

These can be done on their own or as part of events or meetings. The announcing is particularly short, so it is recommended that it be added it to something else.

The next section is about the black mass. Most of these would go well as part of a black mass. The Ending might be an exception though. I think The Wedding in particular would be great as part of a black mass.

𝕿𝖍𝖊 𝕬𝖓𝖓𝖔𝖚𝖓𝖈𝖎𝖓𝖌

(To be performed during meetings or other events as needed)

We are here to share in joy of <name or names>, as they/she announce their/her intentions to us.

Are you announcing your intention to bring a new life into this world?

(I am/We are)

We gladly acknowledge what is to be, and congratulate you on this new addition to your family.

The Welcoming

As previously announced to us, <name(s)> have a brought a new life into this world.

OR

Unbeknownst to us, but welcome nonetheless, <name(s)> have brought a new life into this world.

Please name the new person we are meeting today.

<name>

We welcome you to this world, <name>. May your life be long and happy.

Do you vow to love this child with all your heart for as long as you shall live?

Do you vow to take seriously your role as parents/a parent, and do your best at fulfilling this joyous obligation?

Do you vow to protect and to guide, to nurture and to educate this child to the best of your ability?

Do you vow to raise this child in accordance with the Baphomet Principle and the Core Values of the United Aspects of Satan?

Do you vow to respect the bodily autonomy of this child, and provide care according to our best current understanding of modern science?

Greetings, <name>, it is very nice to meet you, on this, your day of welcoming.

The Transitioning

We are here to mark the passage of time, to note that childhood is at an end, and the transitioning has begun.

We offer our support to <name> as he/she/they embarks on this difficult journey of transition. It is an arduous struggle, a turbulent time of tribulation.

We offer our guidance to <name> during this time of learning and discovery. There are so many changes to come, and so much to learn.

From Lack of understanding to wisdom; from ignorance to knowledge; from darkness to enlightenment.

The transitioning can also be a special time of great joy. Take the time to savor these moments as you progress through the stages of change.

We encourage you to take the left hand path of individualism, and the understanding of self. With that understanding, comes the inner peace that is the catalyst of compassion, wisdom, reason, and a strong sense of justice. We wish all that and more for you, on this, your transitioning.

The Becoming

We are here to acknowledge the time of becoming, the end of the great transition, and to welcome a new adult member of the United Aspects of Satan.

Who stands before me at his/her/their time of becoming?

<name>

This marks the beginning of adulthood, although more maturity is yet to come, over at least another dozen years. With this start of adulthood, you can have full membership, and start the becoming.

It is a journey that never ends. Each day you can become a better person than you were the day before. Therefore you are always becoming, and do not arrive until your last day. May this process be a long and happy one.

The Joining

We are here to welcome a new member to the United Aspects of Satan. You will become a full member and begin the becoming.

Who stands before me to be welcomed as a new member?

<name>

This marks the beginning of your membership, and entering the time of becoming.

It is a journey that never ends. Each day you can become a better person than you were the day before. Therefore you are always becoming, and do not arrive until your last day. May this process be a long and happy one.

The Wedding

Family and Friends of the couple standing before you, we have gathered to witness the commencement of the ultimate level of commitment in the union of these two people. Such is their satisfaction, fulfillment, and joy of the time they have spent together, and likewise the strength of the love each feels toward the other, that they are certain it is time to formally, and legally cement their union.

(Optional section for either a custom ritual or the reading of something meaningful to the couple.)

It is now time to present the rings, which will symbolize the bond between you.

You will both read your vows and then place the ring on the finger of your true love.

(Indicate the person who will go first, have him/her/them read vows, and place the ring. Repeat with the other person.)

Do you, <name>, take this man/woman/person to be your lawfully wedded husband/wife/spouse, (In accordance with the core values of the United Aspects of Satan)?

(Repeat with the other person.)

By the power vested in me by the state of <state> (and the United Aspects of Satan), I now pronounce you <preferred term> and <preferred term>.

You may now have your first kiss as a married couple.

May your love last forever and your days together be filled with happiness and health.

<Optionally the entire thing may be custom if so desired. It can also be done as part of a black mass.>

The Ending

We have gathered here today to commemorate and celebrate a life. This is the ending, and it is something we must all face in time. It is by its very nature, a time of great sorrow. Despite this feeling, we must carry on with the celebration of a life—the life of this person who is so very dear to us.

<custom ritual, meaningful readings, etc.>

It is now time for the remembrance of <name>. We take a moment of silence now to reflect on what <name> meant to us in life, and what we miss in death.

<pause>

Let us now share some memories of <name>.

<people share short stories meaningful in their relationship with the deceased.>

<eulogy specific to the deceased>

Through this reflection and remembrance, we commemorate, and celebrate, the life of <name>, (member of the United Aspects of Satan,) in memoriam.

The Black Mass

The black mass is for entertainment and theatrics more than anything and there is an element of humor and mockery. It can also have a ceremony inserted into it, including one that may contain a custom ritual.

The first step is preparing. You need something to be an altar where a practitioner of some sort can stand behind it, while an audience looks on. Something as simple as a table works—perhaps a folding table with a black and red tablecloth over it.

You need a Chanukah Menorah and nine black candles. This is not to be confused with a standard Temple Menorah, which has only seven candleholders rather than nine. The kosher Chanukah Menorah will have eight candleholders on one level, and additional one on another level. I prefer the one with the lighting candle in the middle, but having it on the side is fine too.

You should have the lighting candle in its place and the other candles lying next to the Menorah. You need something to light the lighting candle with. You need some sort of dish and a chalice or goblet. You may need other smaller dishes, and possibly some little plastic or paper cups.

You need some small crackers of some sort, but nothing greasy or messy. They should have a mild flavor. You need some wine or other preferred beverage. You can get some good wine, or if you are on a budget, you can get kosher wine. Kosher wine is not very expensive and it still tastes good. You may NOT use most of the cheaper wines. That is unacceptable. Box wine is right out. Giving people nasty cheap wine is an abomination. It would make Satan cry if was not for the fact that Satan is imaginary.

I am serious about the crackers. No one wants to deal with that oily shit, or having cheese dust everywhere. Did I mention that cheap wine is a vile insult? Do not do that. If you want a strong wine, get some decent port. Do not get Nighttrain or Thunderbird. That is not even cool—not at all.

If you only have a regular grocery store near you, look for some Mogen David or some Manischewitz. That is probably going to be the only stuff that is at all drinkable in the whole place. Do not torture people with nasty wine.

Get everything set up on the altar and have everyone come sit down. You are now ready to begin.

In the name of the eight infernal aspects, hails and greetings!

People: Hail Satan!

Place the other eight candles into the Menorah. You can go left to right or right to left. Remember which, because you want to light them the other way. So, you will light the last candle you placed first.

Use whatever you brought with you to light the lighting candle. Take the lit candle and hold it up.

Eight archetypes that symbolize eight sets of philosophical concepts, are represented by these eight candles.

Light the candles in the opposite order you placed them, and then put the lighting candle back. After lighting each candle, say one of the lines below, and people will give the response.

Rebellion against arbitrary authority

People: Hail Satan!

Perseverance in the face of opposition

People: Hail Ba'al!

Scientific and philosophical skepticism

People: Hail Lucifer!

The use of logic, reason, and empirical evidence to shape our morality

People: Hail Baphomet!

Community for the creative freedom and betterment of every person

People: Hail Leviathan!

Individualism and individual accomplishment

People: Hail Belial!

Indulgence in the pleasures of life

People: Hail Pan!

The application of humor, fun, wit, and cunning in our endeavors

People: Hail Loki!

You should have a total of nine lit candles now.

Now you announce the first reading. You can read it or have someone else read it after you announce it. The reading should be an essay or a part of an essay. This has United Aspects of Satan material in mind, but obviously, this is made to be customizable.

The first reading is <title, and which part> from <the book or website> by <author's name>.

When the reading is done: *The word of the author.*

People: Thanks, dude.

The Baphomet Principle

Pause for a moment.

Self-motivation balanced with compassion and reason, in all things.

People: Hail Satan!

The second reading is <title, and which part> from <the book or website> by <author's name>.

When the reading is done: *The word of the author.*

People: Thanks, dude.

Do not fill in the name as it was already announced. Literally say the word "author".

Make sure the second reading is from a different essay than the first. A different author is usually good too.

I will now read from The Satanic Narratives.

Pick part of one of the narratives, from which to read. You could maybe read an entire narrative if it is a short one.

This is from the Narrative of <name>

When the reading is done: *Written by Damien Ba'al*

People: Thanks, Damien.

You will need to speak on the topic you just read about, or something else that makes sense. Speak at least one minute. Do not go over five minutes. Two to three minutes is probably the sweet spot.

Get the crackers and wine out. Put it in front of you. Have the crackers in a bowl or on a plate. Have the wine in a bottle. If it is chilled, hopefully it had been in a cooler. Uncork the wine if it has a cork (yes, they make nicer wines with regular lids now. Don't be a snob.) Let the wine breathe a little.

Have some moist towelettes around. Use one to wipe your hands. It should be unnecessary if you followed the instructions on the crackers, but do it anyway.

When that is all done, make the sign of the horns and hold it up.

Ave Satanas!

Lift up your horns!

Everyone makes the sign of the horns and raises them up.

People: "Horns up!"

Pause for a moment, while you and everyone else have the horns up.

Hail Satan!

People: Hail Satan!

Turn your attention back to the crackers. Motion to the crackers.

These are some crackers we pretend are Satan.

People: We pretend.

Grab the bottle of wine, or whatever you are using. During the following speech, you pour some wine into the goblet, chalice, or whatever you have there.

This may look like a bottle of <name the type of wine>, and that is because that is exactly what it is—but I am calling it magic devil piss, because that is what I feel like doing.

Hopefully this stuff all tastes okay, and no one gets indigestion or anything. Well, you shouldn't because I am only giving each person a little.

Have a cracker and drink some wine. Pause for a moment.

Yeah, it is good.

Divide the crackers into different bowls if needed. Have someone help with the wine. Probably best to pour a little in some small disposable cups. Then have people line up. Each person in turn will approach you. You repeat this with everyone. The first person will get a cracker from you. Then they move over in front of the person next to you for some wine.

You can give a cracker to the next person, while the first person is getting wine. This is how it goes for each person.

Hold up a cracker and say: *A cracker you pretend is Satan.*

Person: I pretend.

Give the person the cracker.

They move over to whoever is handing out the wine, while you get the next cracker ready.

The person with the wine grabs a cup and holds it up saying, "magic devil piss".

Person: Hail Satan!

They give the person the cup. The person drinks and disposes of the cup or takes it with them, or whatever you decide.

When everyone is done, you continue to the next part. Make the Vulcan sign where they usually say, "live long and prosper".

May the force be with you!

People: And Doctor Who!

Make the sign of the horns.

Now give each other a hearty hail Satan!

People should make the sign of the horns at each other and say "hail Satan" to each other at the same time. Give everyone a minute or so to do that.

Blow out the Menorah candles like it is a birthday cake.

The black mass has ended. Let us go in peace and reason to indulge in the carnal pleasures of life.

People: Thanks, dude. It was fun.

If you have a ceremony in the black mass, skip the two readings. Just do the Baphomet Principle and read from The Satanic Narratives. Then instead of speaking, do the ceremony.

𝕹otes:

Notes:

Notes:

Epilogue

The idea in writing this book was to provide certain things to members of my organizations, to everyone who reads The Satanic Narratives, and to the Satanic community in general.

The first element is fun and symbolism. That is always an important part of Satanism. People can enjoy doing it and it has a Satanic aesthetic.

Rituals are entirely psychological. I think there should be no woo at all, and they should provide as much real mental health benefit as possible. I want everyone to feel better, happier, and get as much out of life as they can. This is all we get. Satanism embraces indulging in all of life's carnal glory. Good mental health makes one more able to do exactly that.

There are rituals that can be done together. This can strengthen groups, chapters, communities, or however you may organize. This gives people a reason to meet and something they can do together.

These communities can also derive more meaning, and incorporate more cultural elements through the ceremonies. The ceremonies mark the important moments of life for people, which draws everyone closer together. The holidays on the websites can do that as well.

Having rituals, ceremonies, holidays, a shared set of philosophies, and a sense of community provide all that is needed to build a culture. It only takes a group of people to customize and utilize those tools.

This can be used by anyone, much like the Satanic Narratives. There are people who agree with my philosophy in its entirety. Some of them are full members of the United Aspects of Satan and some are not. There are others who agree with a large portion of my philosophy, and adapt it to their purposes. Some people openly talk about this, and for others, with different affiliations, it may be a guarded secret.

The material can be customized by anyone though. This book, and The Satanic Narratives can be used to form your own local group, under your control, customized as you wish, with no connection to me at all. I provide everything needed for that, and hope that it can be useful for others.

There is no such thing as a "one true Satanism". While I wrote this with my members in mind, I also intended it for everyone else, to help them create a praxis that is the true Satanism for them. It is a practical guide to "living the Narratives". I hope it guides you to getting the most out of your praxis.

Hail Satan!

About the Author

Damien Ba'al is a Unix/Linux engineer by day and a philosopher by night. He is a Satanist, a skeptic, a critical thinker, and many other things. Damien lives with his wife and cats, where he enjoys a number of intellectual hobbies. He has a love of learning and of teaching. Active on social media, Damien's words convey his dark presence to all the outcasts and individualists traveling the Left-Hand Path.

https://www.facebook.com/author.damien.baal

https://twitter.com/Damien_Baal @Damien_baal

http://damienbaal.com/

http://uaofsatan.org/

http://atheisticsatanism.com/

Made in the USA
Middletown, DE
01 October 2023

39912590R00156